A compelling narrative on the history of the Kashmir dispute

QUIET FLOWS THE RIVER Jhelum

JAJABOR

Translated from the Bengali original *Jhelum Nodir Tirey* by Sujit Kumar Das

PAPER MISSILE

NIYOGI BOOKS

This English edition is courtesy New Age Publishers (P) Ltd, who are the publishers of the original Bengali novel *Jhelum Nodir Tirey* by Jajabor

Published by
NIYOGI BOOKS
Block D, Building No. 77,
Okhla Industrial Area, Phase-I,
New Delhi-110 020, INDIA
Tel: 91-11-26816301, 26818960
Email: niyogibooks@gmail.com
Website: www.niyogibooksindia.com

Editor: Sukanya Sur
Design: Nabanita Das

ISBN: 978-93-89136-55-5
Publication: 2020
First published Jaistha 1361 (May 1954)

Printed at: Niyogi Offset Pvt. Ltd., New Delhi, India

In the lotus feet of
Sri Phani Bhusan Mukhopadhyay
Smt Manorama Devi

Mountbatten says as a military operation, the speed of the fly-in on the 27th October left our SEAC efforts standing.

—**Allan Campbell Johnson**

Jhelum Nodir Tirey was serialized in the monthly periodical *Mouchak*. Before publication as a book (1954), some portions of it were re-written and some new portions added.

The circulation of the book was stopped in Pakistan-ruled East Bengal (now Bangladesh). Accusing it of 'threat to the stability and security of the state' under the relevant sections of the Security of Pakistan Act, the government there confiscated all copies of the book *Jhelum Nodir Tirey* and banned it.

In 1960, *Jhelum Nodir Tirey* was translated into Hindi and published as a book. The translator was the famous Hindi littérateur Manmath Nath Gupta.

Melting snows of the Himalayas gave birth to the river. Down the mountain slope, past the pine forests, the river meanders its way to the plains. Flowing past the anise fields and the willow groves, the river cuts its course right across the town. Wooden dwellings crowd both the banks, and through the middle flows the languid stream. In darkness, from afar, it resembles the long and slender parting of dark hair of a newly-wed woman.

Jhelum. The petite name is clear and sweet. Golden rays of the morning sun splatter on its bosom. The image of the starry sky shimmers in the evening. The Jhelum sparkles night and day.

The grand royal palace made of milky white marble rises right on the river bank. Sepoys and sentries stand guard at the entrance and the stairway. Liveried guardsmen carry out flag marches in the courtyard.

In the olden days, this used to be the main palace of the king. The old Maharaja had spent his life here. The new king was cut from a different cloth. He had shifted to the new 'English'-style palace built on the hillside, along with his family and servants. There, the oil lamp was replaced by the electric bulb and the elephant shed had given way to the motor garage.

The old palace had lately been converted into a government office. From there, the designated officials rule over, or rather rip off the subjects in the name of the king. The royal durbar was convened at the central hall only twice a year. The old palace woke up to its former pomp and glory. The Maharaja arrived in his palanquin along with the royal entourage to the beating of drums and the sound of bugles.

The Dussehra Durbar was the biggest festivity of the country and the greatest gala of the year.

Maharaja Hari Singh, the absolute monarch of Kashmir, was sitting on the brocaded ivory throne underneath the bejewelled canopy. His bodyguard was standing below, holding an unsheathed sword. Behind the throne stood another attendant holding the umbrella. Eight servants stood on either side of the throne, swaying the fans. A golden oil lamp was glowing on the silver stand; perfumed incense was burning in the stone incense burner from Jaipur. The royal entourage in their finery occupied the front row. Behind them were seated other notables according to their rank. The durbar hall was dazzling with flowers and zari decorations and multicoloured lights.

But amidst such grandeur, the Maharaja appeared downcast. Why was a smile missing from his face? Why weren't his eyes twinkling with pleasure?

In fact, the Maharaja was not happy at all.

It was only two months since the British had left India. While departing, they had divided the country into two, handing over one part to the Muslims. They were bitterly opposed to the Hindus, so much so that they refused to live in the same country. The Muslim country carved out of India was named Pakistan.

No sooner had the British left India than almost all the princely states merged with the country that they shared their boundaries with. Jaipur, Gwalior, Cooch Behar, and others merged with India, while Bahawalpur and Kalat acceded to Pakistan. Kashmir was still undecided.

It was contiguous with both India and Pakistan. On the west, the boundary with Pakistan runs for twenty-five miles, while in the south-east, its boundary merges with India. Which country would Kashmir merge with? The Maharaja was indecisive. After much reflection, he finally said, 'Joining neither country for the time being. Let's stay put. We will decide it later.'

Whatever be the Maharaja's position, others were not willing to wait. The Indian leaders were not forthcoming on the issue, but on the other side, the Pakistani bosses were restive. They wanted immediate control over Kashmir. The Maharaja of Kashmir was a Hindu, Dogra Rajput. The subjects of the state were mostly Muslims. The ranking leaders of Pakistan shook their heads and said, 'This is intolerable'. Taking the cue, the lower rung clenched their fists and roared, 'We will take it by force!'

True to their words, they started off with an economic blockade. They hit where it hurt the most.

Kashmir was a mountainous state where agriculture was the mainstay. Paddy in the fields and fruits in the orchards –

these were about the only produce there. All of the rest had to be procured from outside. It arrived on the road from Lahore or Rawalpindi. Pakistan stopped the supplies. As a result, motor vehicles stopped plying on the roads of Kashmir for want of petrol, classes stopped in schools and colleges for want of paper, sweetmeat trays in the shops remained empty for want of sugar. The patients in the state could not get medicines nor the children their food. Even the poor workingmen swallowed their rice with difficulty for lack of salt.

But that was just the beginning. Like the incarceration before hanging, tongue-lash before the beating, the forcible raids started from early September. Almost every day, bands of Pakistanis entered Kashmiri villages from across the border for loot and rampage.

The situation had further deteriorated during the last four days. News had arrived that like regular soldiers, thousands of invaders had launched an attack on Kashmir. They had crossed the border with the enemy territory at various places and captured scores of villages. Their largest band was advancing in lorries towards Domel, on the way to Srinagar. The band consisted of a thousand tribes from the North-West Frontier Province, hundreds of Pathan Afridis, and countless Muslim League volunteers, and had named themselves Muslim National Guard.

The princely states had so long been depending upon the British government in times of trouble. Their own troops were too few to reckon with. Kashmiri troops were only a few in number, half of whom were Muslims. As the enemy invaded, they too deserted. Let alone putting up any resistance, they joined the invaders shouting, 'Allah Hu Akbar!' 'Biting the hand that feeds you' - goes the popular saying. These traitors guided the intruders towards Srinagar. Any wonder that the Maharaja was upset?

The Maharaja could not help but attend the Dussehra Durbar. The tradition was continuing for the last hundred years since the time of Maharaja Gulab Singh. The precedent set by the ancestors could scarcely be broken. Hence, the durbar had to be called this time too.

At the durbar, the family priest chanted mantras. The court poet composed and sang songs in praise of the Maharaja. Restraining his anxiety, the king bestowed titles to some and honours to others. The nobles placed their tributes at the feet of the king, one after the other. Some paid five gold coins, others two – as was customarily fixed from the time of their forefathers. Of the landlords and feudatories, some gifted richly embroidered cerulean woollen coats, while others presented baskets full of musk or the horns of the famed bharal (blue sheep) of Gilgit.

Suddenly, the city police chief entered the durbar in a hurry and said something to the mayor in a hushed tone. An alarmed mayor rose to whisper something to his superior who, in turn, relayed it to his senior. Then the secret was conveyed to the minister who told it with trepidation to the diwan. An ashen-faced diwan went up to the king and broke the bad news.

After hearing the news, Maharaja Hari Singh remained speechless for a while. Then he abruptly rose from the throne and went out with the diwan. This time, he shunned the palanquin and speeded off in his motor car to the new palace.

The court members looked at each other in utter surprise. What was the matter? A little later, it became known that the matter was serious. Bad news travel fast. Brigadier Rajendra Singh had died in battle. That was calamitous!

Rajendra Singh was the Maharaja's Chief Commander. He was valiant and courageous. The Maharaja completely depended upon him. The Hindu troops that still remained in the Kashmir army numbered around a hundred and fifty. Rajendra Singh went ahead with them to stop the intruders.

The intruders had advanced till Uri, sixty-five miles from Srinagar. There, Rajendra Singh confronted the enemy with his modest number of troops. He and his soldiers fought without so much as a thought for their own lives. The intruders were ten times their number. Rajendra Singh restrained them at Uri for two whole days with extraordinary valour. Then he died in the battle along with his soldiers. How long could one hundred and fifty fight against one and a half thousand?

From the king's court, the news spread everywhere by word of mouth. Shops downed their shutters, streets became empty, men and women cowered in their homes out of fear. Nobody knew what lay in store for the day hereafter.

But they did not get even a night's respite. At around ten in the night, the lights of the city went out all of a sudden. The power station was at Mahura where the water of a mountain stream was harnessed to produce electricity. The electricity was transported to far-flung cities through cables fixed on poles. After reaching Mahura, the intruders had smashed the machinery there into pieces.

Mahura was only fifty miles from the capital. That came as a shock. How safe was Srinagar? A smooth metalled road runs by Mahura. How long would it take for the truck full of intruders to arrive in Srinagar by that road? Was there any hope left? People started fleeing the city for dear life from that very night. They rode on motor car, lorry, horse-drawn carriages, bullock carts, cycles, or horses to escape in different directions. Those who had no other means started walking with their family in search of a safe haven.

At the palace, Hari Singh let out a deep sigh and asked, 'Diwan, what's the way out?'

The diwan replied with folded hands, 'Maharaj, only the Indian government can save us. Ask for their help.'

A year back, he did not allow Pandit Nehru to enter his state and had had him arrested. The king had kept that in mind. The same Nehru was now the head of the Indian government. He asked anxiously, 'Will they respond?'

The diwan replied, 'My Lord, to protect the afflicted is the dharma of a human; if they do not do so, then what makes them virtuous? To resist the tormentor is the mandate of justice; if they do not follow that, then what makes them rulers? You send the appeal. Any further delay will be disastrous.'

Then in the darkened palace, in his personal chamber, Hari Singh, the last Maharaja of Kashmir, sat down and wrote the letter himself in the light of a lamp. It was a fervent appeal to the new government of India. He wrote, 'Send the army immediately and protect Kashmir. For God's sake, save its four million inhabitants.'

The date was 25 October 1947.

Back in New Delhi, the Maharaja's wire had set Prime Minister Nehru thinking about the next course of action. The Deputy Prime Minister Sardar Vallabhbhai Patel and other ministers wanted the troops despatched to Kashmir to stop the intruders. But the Governor General Lord Mountbatten was extremely reluctant. He was now only the titular head and was relegated to an advisory role. He said, 'What if Pakistan too sends its troops to aid the invaders?'

The general and the army brass, all Englishmen, were summoned. They shook their heads gravely and said that it's dangerous to send troops to Kashmir. The cabinet held their ground and countered that it was cowardly to let fear come in the way of aiding the Maharaja. Besides, the Pakistanis should never be allowed to capture Kashmir by force.

True, but Kashmir had yet to accede to India, and if law be respected, then it is not incumbent upon the Indian government to protect it.

When the word got around to Maharaja Hari Singh, he promptly signed the Instrument of Accession on the following day and joined the Indian Union for good.

Thereafter, the Indian government ordered the general to send troops to Kashmir.

There was only one road from Delhi to Kashmir, and it lay over mountains, across rivers, and through jungles. It was almost three hundred miles long, and that too in bad shape. At places, it was too steep for cars to climb, and elsewhere, too narrow for two people to walk abreast. Proceeding along that road would defeat the very purpose. The invaders would overrun Kashmir before the Indian troops could arrive. So, airlifting the troops was the only way out.

The troops stationed at Delhi cantonment were not enough. A battalion of the Sikh Regiment was stationed at Gurgaon twelve miles away. On getting the orders, a part of them arrived at Palam Airport under the cover of darkness. They were somehow attired and equipped in haste. On 27 October, as the morning star faded and a pale glow lit up the eastern sky, the engines of three air force Dakotas roared to life. They sailed towards Kashmir with the Sikh soldiers on board. That was the first mission of the armed forces of independent India.

The troops were airborne, but would they be able to land in Srinagar? What if the airport there had already been captured by the invaders? Everyone at the headquarters in Delhi were seized with that concern. The wire and telephone people were sitting before their equipment, headphones firmly in place. The top brass was enquiring every half an hour whether any news had arrived. None so far.

It was past nine. No news yet. Nine-thirty, ten … no news yet. Quarter past ten, twenty, twenty-five … the clock kept on ticking past the minutes, each of which felt like an age. None spoke; the silence in the room became oppressive. Everyone was almost choking with tension. Why was the news taking so long to arrive? Had the worst already happened? It's ten-thirty, thirty-one … suddenly, the light glowed on the wireless board.

'Hello, hello, Delhi, hello – this is Srinagar calling, hello?' The news had arrived. The three Dakotas had landed safely. The Indian army had reached Kashmir for the first time. Hurray!

The top bosses let out a collective sigh of relief and remarked, 'Thank God, the merciful.'

The Sikh contingent that flew into Srinagar was headed by Lt Colonel Dewan Ranjit Rai. The surname sounds Bengali, isn't it? Actually, he was a Punjabi – almost six feet tall, thirty-six-inch chest, square wrists hewn out of steel. A figure meant to give a good fight.

He was briefed to secure the airport with his small detachment of soldiers. Not to fight till enough troops and ammunitions are placed at his disposal.

At the airport, Colonel Rai was taken aback on hearing about the situation in Kashmir. The enemy had captured the town of Baramulla near Srinagar. If they advanced a little more and crossed the hilly region, they could fan out through the plains and villages and surround Srinagar from all sides.

It was a real possibility. The number of invaders, their location, or equipment were unknown. Without this knowledge, it would be suicidal to engage with the enemy with only a hundred soldiers. But to wait for reinforcements would mean giving up on Srinagar. Colonel Rai faced a real quandary.

There was no time to think things out. A minute wasted meant letting the enemy advance one more gauge. Colonel Rai straightaway arrived at a decision. Whatever be the instructions from Delhi, if the invaders were not intercepted right away, everything would be lost. He got his soldiers ready.

Another problem cropped up. How would the soldiers move? They neither had any military truck, nor jeep, nor any other form of transport. Some of the motor buses that plied people and goods on the roads of Srinagar were commandeered for the purpose. Colonel Rai and his troops proceeded on them.

Two miles east of Baramulla lay a small hill, alongside which runs the metalled road to Srinagar. Two hundred gauge from there flows the river Jhelum. Colonel Rai took position on top of that hill. As the enemy invaders approached, he ordered, 'Fire!' The rifles of the Sikh soldiers blazed in unison–rat-tat-tat!

The invaders had come this far from Uri without facing any resistance. The sudden hail of bullets took them by surprise. The ones in front fell like ninepins on both sides of the road. The ones at the rear chaotically fell back here and there.

At last, they took positions and launched a counter-attack.

Colonel Rai realized shortly that whatever he had heard was not true. Many in Delhi were of the opinion that the invaders were a ragtag group of hooligans, out to loot and plunder, armed with swords, cleavers, lances, crackers, and muzzle-loading guns. Not at all. They knew all the artifices of modern warfare. They were knowledgeable enough about dividing themselves into small units and sub-units and carrying out warfare. They were under the command of trained leaders like captain, major, and colonel. They possessed Bren guns, Sten guns, light and heavy machine guns, hand grenades, anti-tank rifles, and various other British weapons. They weren't the ones to run off on seeing army fatigues and flags.

The Sikh soldiers were minuscule in number as compared to the intruders. But there was a big advantage in taking position on top of the hill. One can fire the gun, undetected. With that advantage, they kept on shooting down the enemy.

The fighting continued for hours. The sun had set and darkness descended. Colonel Rai noticed that a group of invaders was sneaking up from the other side of the hill. That was alarming. If the enemy entraps them from both sides, none of the Sikh soldiers would come out alive. He realized that his troops had to be moved at once in order to save them. So he ordered them to retreat.

Clicking heels, the head constable saluted him and asked, 'Huzur, what about you?'

The colonel smiled and said that the enemy had to be restrained with gunfire, so that they do not catch up from behind. And he will be the last one to move. A captain was not supposed to leave the battlefield till the last of his soldiers was moved to safety. This was his firm conviction. He kept on firing from his machine gun.

The Sikh soldiers continued to retreat. But the invaders were not sitting idle either. Bullets from their blazing guns rained around the colonel and his soldiers. Some of them fell to the bullets and a few were wounded. Within an hour, the remaining soldiers reached a safe position, evading the invaders.

At last, Colonel Rai rose, only to be felled by a bullet that pierced the darkness to hit him on the forehead. Hero Ranjit Rai died a soldier's death while fighting on the battlefield.

Ranjit Rai had passed out of the Dehradun Military College thirteen years before and joined the Indian army as a second lieutenant. He had earned a name in the last World War, fighting the Japanese in the jungles of Burma. Promotion wasn't late in coming. From lieutenant to captain, and then to major and lieutenant colonel. A promising career was cut short by his untimely death at the age of thirty-four. A tender fruit had fallen to the ground before it could ripen.

Colonel Rai took untimely leave of this many-splendoured earth. But he died to save Srinagar and the state of Kashmir. Lakhs of men, women, and children were kept out of harm's way. The invaders were sundered by the charge of the Sikh regiment. They were no more in a position to advance further.

In death, Colonel Rai and his comrades gained immortality. Those who travel on the road to Baramulla would come across a memorial plaque placed on the side of the hill. The wooden board bore the legend in English – 'In eternal remembrance of the brave Sikh soldiers of India who laid down their lives while fighting the invaders here on 27th October 1947 and secured the independence of Kashmir.'

There is another stone monument in Kashmir, surrounded by a wooden fence. The English plaque there might be given a miss because even an illiterate farmer would know the name that the memorial bore. Bowing before it, he would touch his forehead and say, 'Colonel Rai was a real hero. He was the one who saved us.'

At the palace in Karachi, the emperor's slumber was getting interrupted. In reality, it was not Karachi but Abbotabad, and not a slumber but a dream. Kashmir was the long cherished dream of Janab Jinna, the *shahensha* of Pakistan. That it was about to be fulfilled was no longer in doubt. Thousands of invaders were equipped and many lorries, trucks, and gallons of petrol were placed at their disposal. They were already in Patan and would advance towards Srinagar. It was going to be a cakewalk.

The new badshah had therefore moved from Karachi to Abbotabad, advancing halfway along to await the happy tidings. The biggest festival of Islam, Id ul-Fitr, marking the end of the Ramzan fasting, was nearing. On that holy day, with the blessings of Hazrat Muhammad, the Quaid-e-Azam of Pakistan, the second largest Islamic state in the world, would march into Kashmir as the conqueror. He would offer his prayers at the head of the congregation at Hazratbal Mosque.

But what's the news coming through? That the invading forces had been intercepted by the Indian Army near Srinagar. So near, yet so far! It was too hard to believe.

Pakistan was confident that before any help could reach across the inhospitable terrain, the Maharaja's army would be cut down and the Pakistani flag would be unfurled from the mast over Kashmir government offices. That the Indian Army would fly into Kashmir within hours was inconceivable on the part of Pakistani leaders.

Jinnah had hardly faced a bigger disappointment in life. His anger breached all limits. He called the Military Secretary to the Governor of Punjab and ordered, 'Call the Commander-in-Chief General Gracey now and convey my orders to march upon Kashmir with the entire Pakistani army, this very moment.'

The general was dumbstruck on hearing this peculiar order. Almost the entire ruling class during the British rule was hostile towards India. The Indian National Congress was the root cause behind their downfall. So they would be only too pleased to destroy the Congress. Be that as it may, but they couldn't go overboard about it. They knew that to arm, equip, and direct a proxy army was one thing; but to launch an open war was a different ball game altogether. Sensing trouble, Gracey said with all respect, 'Your Excellency, I am subordinate to Sir Auchinleck. What can I do without his orders?'

That was true. During partition, both the nations had consented to Auchinleck becoming their chief of staff. India and Pakistan had their separate commander-in-chiefs in Lieutenant General Sir Rob Lockhart and Douglas Gracey respectively.

On top of them was the common supreme commander, Field Marshal Sir Claude Auchinleck.

Hearing the news, Auchinleck dashed to Lahore by air. He told Jinnah that sending the Pakistani army to Kashmir meant war with India, and that would be disastrous.

Jinnah argued that the army of Hindustan had come to Kashmir to aid the Hindu Maharaja. Hence, the Pakistan army would go in to help the Muslims there.

Auchinleck said, 'Kashmir had joined the Indian union by signing the Instrument of Accession. Therefore, Kashmir is now a part of India, whose defence is the responsibility of the Indian government. It is perfectly legal for the Indian army to go and fight there.'

'Instrument of Accession? But that's a load of rubbish and fraud,' roared Jinnah. 'Kashmir's accession to India is just a staged event.'

Auchinleck could pacify him only after a lot of reasoned arguments and deliberations. The governor general of Pakistan finally rescinded his order to send troops to Kashmir. On the advice of Auchinleck, Jinnah wrote to Mountbatten, inviting him and Nehru to come to Pakistan. The three of them would sit and discuss so as to arrive at a solution to the Kashmir problem.

While a restrained letter was sent to Delhi, an intemperate statement was issued to the press. India had annexed Kashmir under the guise of Instrument of Accession. Pakistan will never accept it. The Muslims there should never be allowed to be subjugated by the Hindustani guns.

The council of ministers in Delhi stood firm. After receiving Jinnah's letter, they asked, 'What problem are they talking about? If it's about the invasion in Kashmir, let them recall the invaders they had sent. And that will be the end of the problem. What's there to deliberate over? Where's the scope for deliberation?

But Mountbatten was eager to make a compromise by any means. He wanted to honour Jinnah's invitation.

Some members of the cabinet commented sarcastically, 'This invitation sounds all too familiar – Hitler meeting Chamberlain on the question of Sudetenland. Only the venue has changed from Berlin to Lahore.'

It was difficult to counter such insinuations. After much deliberation, it was decided that only Mountbatten would go to Lahore. The two governors general would meet at the Governor's Palace in Lahore.

After the exchange of pleasantries, Jinnah said, 'Pakistan was kept in the dark about the Indian government's intention to send troops to Kashmir.'

Mountbatten replied, 'That can't be. The first thing that Nehru did after coming out of the cabinet meeting, where it was decided to airlift troops to Kashmir, was to telegram the Pakistani Prime Minister Liaquat Ali.'

Jinnah changed the question and straightaway asked, 'How dare India send troops to another country?'

'In exercise of the powers conferred by the Instrument of Accession,' replied Mountbatten.

Jinnah said gravely, 'Kashmir's accession to India was a fraud.'

'No, it is an absolute fact,' insisted Mountbatten.

Jinnah was derisive, 'Did the two-and-a-half million Muslims in Kashmir plead for it before the Indian government?'

Mountbatten said, 'That was not necessary in law. The Maharaja himself had signed the instrument.'

Jinnah countered, 'Maharaja? Who was he to sign it? The people of the princely state are the sole arbiters on the question of accession to India or Pakistan.'

Mountbatten smirked silently, as if saying to himself, 'Mr Jinnah, how come, in the case of Junagarh, you people had said that the will of the nawab was the last word in law with regard to accession?'

Jinnah possibly read Mountbatten's lips. He said firmly, 'We will never accept Kashmir's accession to India. It was done forcibly.'

Mountbatten calmly replied, 'Very true. And that force was applied by the invaders. They are the ones behind the aggression in Kashmir. And Pakistan is responsible for that.'

The discussion kept moving in circles, between the same set of accusations and refutations.

Finally, Jinnah said, 'Let us come to a settlement. Let both the sides withdraw from Kashmir immediately.'

Mountbatten argued, 'Granted that the onus lie upon India to bring back its troops. But who will ensure that the invaders return?'

Jinnah said, 'Once you withdraw the Indian soldiers, we will take steps to rein in the invaders.'

Take note! So long Pakistan had been protesting that the invaders in Kashmir were frontier tribesmen, that they were not under Pakistani control. Such posturing was only for public consumption. Privately, they are not averse to acknowledging the truth.

The discussion ended, but the argument did not. The problem was not resolved. The hostility between the two newly formed nations continued unabated.

Mountbatten and Jinnah took leave of each other with all official formality, untouched by personal warmth.

A Bengali officer, Brigadier L.P. Sen came to lead the war in Kashmir. Not Labannya Prasad or Lalit Prasanna, but Lionel Pratip Sen. Like his name, Lionel Pratip wasn't born here either. His father was a renowned barrister in Burma. He was born in Rangoon and had studied in a British convent there. After graduating from Sandhurst in Britain, he had joined the Indian army as an officer about a year before the last World War.

Distinguished Service Order is one of the top awards in the army, bestowed for exemplary courage under fire. In the last war, Brigadier Sen was the commander of the 10th Baluch Regiment. He received the award for defeating the Japanese army in the jungles of Cong in Burma.

Arriving in Srinagar, Brigadier Sen found that the enemy was trying to capture the capital from two sides. One column, leading the frontal attack, was driving down the metalled road from Baramulla in motor trucks, sporting green flags with the moon and star insignia. The other column attacking from the left was creeping up along the village road on foot. Two powerful detachments were trying to hold the city in a death grip from two sides like the jaws of a serpent and swallow it gradually.

Brigadier Sen realized that he needed a few days' time to start with. He had to stave off the advancing invaders for the time being. Routing them could wait for another day.

The first priority was to secure the airport eight miles outside the city. It was the only link between Kashmir and India. Losing it meant shutting the door to all traffic from India.

A Garhwali regiment had flown into Srinagar. Brigadier Sen deployed some of them to guard the airport. They patrolled round the clock with rifles slung on their shoulders. None was admitted without a pass. They would holler, 'Hu-kum-dar?' to anybody found loitering around in such a coarse voice that it would give a jolt.

After a sleepless night, as the dawn broke, the invaders started trickling into Budgam, a village only half a mile from the airport. It was just a hailing distance away; that near.

The battle started between the Garhwali troops and the invading forces. It was a close hand-to-hand combat. The enemy, numbering around seven hundred, attacked with grenade and Bren gun. The Garhwalis, only half in number, counter-attacked with rifles. Fierce fighting continued for four hours. Black smoke from the bursting ammunition clouded the sky, its report deafening the ear. The ground darkened with the blood of the dead and the dying.

The invaders in their desperation bore down upon the Garhwalis in waves. And each time the waves were thwarted after touching the shore. They failed to dislodge the Garhwalis from their position.

As the news reached Brigadier Sen in Srinagar, he quickly dispatched more troops, arms, and ammunition. The invaders were already gasping for breath. They did not have the stomach to fight the new arrivals. Two hundred of the enemy were killed in no time. The rest thought that it was best to retreat. The danger was lifted from the Srinagar airport.

The victory at Budgam was a signal achievement for the Garhwal regiment. But their commander Major Somnath Sharma was killed in the fighting. He led his soldiers from the front. The joy of victory paled in grief over his death.

But commanders could ill afford to sit and mourn the dead. How can a doctor treat if he is upset over a patient's death? Brigadier Sen engaged himself in defending Kashmir. Tents were pitched in the open field to make barracks for the soldiers, and ammunition depots were built with sandbags. Deodar trunks were erected as telephone poles to connect the various offices.

Soldiers and even more soldiers had to be airlifted to Kashmir, and without delay. But that required a fleet of aircraft, which was not there. That set the top brass thinking at the army headquarters in Delhi.

Suddenly, it occurred that quite a few private airlines were operating within the country. They operated daily flights between important cities like Kolkata, Bombay, Delhi, Guwahati, and others, ferrying both passengers and goods. They had about a hundred airplanes between them – mostly

Dakotas. Through a government diktat, all of them were acquired and flown to Delhi overnight. They started ferrying troops and war supplies round the clock to Srinagar from the two airports at Palam and Safdarjung.

Pilot, radio officer, ground engineer, and crew – none had a moment's respite. The sorties began at the crack of dawn and the planes returned one after the other at dusk. The day came to an end, but the chores did not. Preparation for the next day started forthwith.

All night long, the porters hauled and stacked the provisions, while the staff members prepared the inventories. Fitters and mechanics went about oiling and cleaning the engine and propeller of the airplanes. There was hardly any time for grub, let alone time to catch forty winks.

Everyone was all praise for these airmen for their boundless energy, working days on end. They were patronizingly called 'machines'.

Indeed, the supply lines functioned with clockwork precision. Arms and ammunition, provisions and platoons continued to arrive at Srinagar by air, just as the ducks and cranes from Manasarovar flock to the plains during fall.

Enthusiasm is no less contagious than infections. Everyone wants to outshine the other. When the air force could display such grit, could the armoured divisions sit idle? That's preposterous. They prayed to their high command for permission to dispatch one-armoured division immediately to Kashmir.

Armoured cars, as the name suggests, are cannons mounted on motor cars and wrapped all around with thick metal plates. The long range of the cannon is ably matched by the speed of the car, intimidating enough to make the enemy run for cover.

But how would the armoured cars move on the road that had thwarted the infantry? Their roofs might get stuck in the dense forest, or their wheels could lose traction over the rocks. The rickety wooden bridges over the streams might give way under the weight of the cannons.

The sappers and miners said that they would go out in front of the armoured cars to make roads for them by hacking off the trees and cutting through the rocks. The MES (Military Engineer Services) people were all engineers. Not to be outdone, they declared that they would embank the ravines and build sturdy bridges.

That sealed the deal. They started from Delhi that very night.

Cutting across the fields of Pathankot, crossing over the peaks of the Pir Panjal, and burrowing through the tunnel at Banihal, an armoured division reached Srinagar one fine morning. Both the young and the old were elated and buoyed seeing the convoy of armoured cars pass by. Lining both sides of the road, they cried out, 'Long live India!', 'Long live Pandit Nehru!'

The remaining days of October went by and November arrived. The first signs of winter appeared in Kashmir. Mist gathered on Hari Parbat. The chinar leaves of Naseem Bagh had turned golden. The roadside walnut trees shed their fruits to reveal bare branches. The cormorants were done with their water sports in Dal Lake. Sitting on the bank, they lazed away the day, spreading their wings towards the warm sunlight.

It was Friday, the 7th of November. Even before the darkness of night had lifted, General Sen issued the order, 'Forward march!'

For the last few days, Brigadier Sen and his fellow officers had completed the preparation for attack. The surroundings of Srinagar were dotted with small hills. There, somewhere, the enemy had positioned themselves. He had made a reconnaissance of the area and mapped out the miles, the forests, pathways, and gorges. Up until then, the Indian army had fought to defend themselves. Now was the time for attack.

Most of the intruders were still fast asleep in their camps along the road from Pattan to Srinagar. Only a handful had risen from sleep. The offensive operations started just then.

The ringleader of the intruders was still in bed. While his partisans were frenzied with their looting during the last few days, their leader was equally ecstatic about the impending victory. He hadn't heard from the Indian soldiers ever since the skirmish at Budgam.

The intruders had gradually advanced from Baramulla to Pattan, unchallenged. And from Pattan to Selatong, which was almost within knocking distance from Srinagar. The capital city was within reach, like a red apple, ripe for the picking. The ringleader had been celebrating with his camp followers late into the night – at times stroking his moustache or caressing his beard with pleasure.

He had fallen into a deep slumber just before dawn. In his dream, he had captured Srinagar, killed the king, and made the Maharani his mistress. Reclined on a pillow, he was smoking scented tobacco from a golden hookah. Just then, the Indian troops launched a fierce attack. He sat up with a jolt and mumbled, 'What! Attack?'

Rubbing his eyes, he took a look around and barked, 'Get me a gun!' But none was around to comply. In the melee, some scrambled for their weapons, others for their clothes, and the rest were running about in confusion, bumping into each other and hurting themselves. Many were slaughtered before they could make out what was happening.

Brigadier Sen had sent one group of soldiers to the north and another to the south. The main infantry remained in the middle. They launched a three-pronged attack on the intruders. How long could the intruders withstand such a pincer attack? They were overpowered within a few hours. On top of that –

What's that? Sounds quite like a machine gun. The raiders looked around in distress. Hell, no! That was an armoured car. It was rushing forth, all guns blazing, raising a cloud of dust. Bullets flew thick and fast. The intruders cried 'Ya Allah!', turned tail, and ran like mad.

Their commander was in a bind. If his men started deserting in this manner, whom will he put up the fight with? He tried to reason with them. He said, 'Brothers, why are you retreating? Have faith that these Indian infidels will be crushed soon. We will capture Srinagar in no time. Long live jihad!'

But none was ready to give heed to it. They said, 'To hell with your Srinagar. It's enough if we can escape with our lives, jihad be damned!' And they scampered in whichever direction they could.

But with the Indian soldiers closing in from three sides, they could barely escape. The only way out was to retreat in the direction that they came from and had advanced towards Srinagar. They dashed that way, leaving behind some of the loot, some arms and ammunition, and about three hundred dead comrades. They ran for dear life, all the way from Selatong to Pattan and from there to Baramulla.

Flushed with victory, the Indian soldiers gave the intruders a chase. But the ordinary public buses were not up to the task.

The army drivers tried their best and floored the accelerator. The speedometer needle jumped from forty to fifty and from there to fifty-five. The window panes of the bus, packed with troops, started rattling. The driver held the steering even more firmly.

The Indian commander shouted, 'Speed, more speed!' The fleeing enemy was now within sight. A few more paces and they could be captured. 'Driver, drive harder, harder!' The needle climbed up to fifty-seven, sixty, sixty-two … a bit more. And then clang, clang, clang! The bus gradually decelerated and came to a halt. What's the matter? Had the engine stalled? The driver cranked the handle to start the bus and pulled the choke. Then he lifted the bonnet to check the engine bay. The petrol had exhausted; not a drop was left.

The intruders fled far away from Baramulla.

But invaders had rarely, if ever, left any country without committing murder and loot. The intruders too left behind a trail of death and destruction all over Baramulla. They had raided the town at midday when the townspeople were busy with their work. The marketplace was humming with activity. Winnowing was going on in the fields. In the court, the clerks were busy drawing petitions in Urdu, glasses fixed on their nose. The wizened maulvi was caressing his white beard while teaching Urdu to his students at the madrasa.

After capturing the town, they fanned out in bands all over the place. It was like locusts descending upon a field of ripened crops. Within a couple of hours, everything lay in ruins.

They started with indiscriminate looting. Cash boxes and safes were broken to loot money and valuables. Jewellery was snatched from women. Brass utensils were taken away from the impoverished who had no other possessions. By evening, they had set the grain silos on fire and cheered in macabre mirth. They jokingly said to one another, '*Badi acchi roshni ho rahi hai* (Wow! Such a brilliant lighting)!'

Not content with looting, they immediately slaughtered any Hindu or Sikh that they came across. Young or old, men or women – the killing went on indiscriminately. Husbands were beheaded in front of their wives; children in their mothers' laps were pierced by bullets. Those who hid in the jungle were spared their lives, but did not escape unhurt.

Pakistan had always termed its invasion of India as jihad (holy war). The Kashmiri subjects were mostly Muslims, while the Maharaja was a Hindu. He allegedly tortured the Muslims all too often. This had enraged the Muslim tribesmen into attacking Kashmir to save their brethren. This was not just another war - it was jihad. They were not invaders but mujahid or holy warriors. That was the assertion of the Pakistani leaders.

But the mujahids did not spare the Muslims of Baramulla. Instead of being saved, they were slaughtered. Besides the many unknown Muslims who were either looted or killed, there was one Maqbool Sherwani, a renowned leader of Baramulla. He was hailed by one and all as a saviour to the distressed and a friend in need. One couldn't praise him enough.

But the Pakistanis nursed a grudge against him for long. Maqbool Sherwani had once rubbed the *shahenshah* of Pakistan, Muhammad Ali Jinnah, the wrong way. Jinnah came to Kashmir a few years back and was addressing a public gathering in Baramulla. He said, 'Let the Muslims of Kashmir unite in the name of Allah, faith, and party.'

Sherwani, who was present there, rose up and said, 'Unite, we will, but why just the Muslims? Let the Hindu, Muslim, Sikh, Buddhist, Jain, Parsi, and the Christian unite too. Let all the people of Kashmir unite.'

Jinnah said indignantly, 'Hindus are infidels and enemy of the Muslims.' Maqbool Sherwani replied, 'Hindus are fellow humans and brothers to the Muslims.'

Jinnah became furious with rage. He walked out of the meeting haughtily without uttering another word. The garlands remained unused and the acclamation unuttered.

The Pakistanis did not forget the incident. They got their revenge now. The invaders tied Sherwani up and brought him before their leader. They ordered, 'Salute him.' He smiled and replied, 'I only bow before my elders.' The flunkies were outraged by his audacity.

Suppressing his indignation, the chief said, 'We have conquered Kashmir and will occupy Srinagar in a day or two. Join us and help in the effort.'

Sherwani defiantly replied, 'It is the duty of every Kashmiri to thwart the invader. Just go to hell, you robbers.'

Everybody burst out in rage. Some wanted his head; others wanted him to be fed to the dogs.

The chief ordered, 'Take him to the crossroads and give him seven hundred lashes. If that doesn't make the fool see reason, then blow his brains out.'

Sherwani was shackled and tied with a rope and dragged to the town square. The intruders gathered all around to have fun.

Sherwani was unperturbed. The lashes hit his back and shoulder, face and chest, cut through his skin, and drenched him in blood.

The minions curtly told him, 'There's still time to save yourself. Just tell if you are willing to join us and say – long live Pakistan!'

Maqbool Sherwani was in no position to speak loudly. His tongue was drying up and he was losing consciousness. In a thin voice, he somehow uttered, 'Long live my beloved Kashmir!'

The next moment, three gunshots cracked from three sides, targeting his head. The intruders' voices rose in celebration – just punishment for the obstinate and a lesson for others.

But there weren't enough people around to learn the lesson. The intruders had done a good job of slaughtering them.

Yet, there were some who had to learn it the hard way. They were not Kashmiris, but foreigners. There was a Christian missionary convent in Baramulla by the name of Presentation Convent.

Long back, an English woman came to Kashmir. She was a Roman Catholic sister, pledged to celibacy and renunciation.

Her heart was filled with sorrow, seeing the suffering of the peasants and workers of Kashmir. She decided to dedicate her life in the service of the poor people here, leaving behind her country, society, and near ones. She voluntarily took up the cause of alleviating the pain and suffering of the people of an unknown land, so far away from home. With her meagre resources, she established this Presentation Convent. Its modest size and resources concealed its large-heartedness.

Years later, the convent had gradually grown bigger with the munificence of pious and generous foreigners – like a giant tree, sprouting from a small seed, spreads its branches and covers itself with flowers. Today, the Presentation Convent boasted of a hospital where hundreds of sick people are given medicine. It has a school for underprivileged children. A workshop for women imparted training in weaving, needlework, embroidery, and handicrafts.

The revered founder had departed. But she had left behind her work and her ideals. Her work had been carried forward by young nuns who had arrived from different countries. They were French, German, and Italian, hailing from different cultures, speaking different languages but united by the common ideal of service to mankind.

Many in the convent were upset after knowing that the invaders were arriving in Baramulla. Mother Superior assured them, 'Let them come. We care for the sick and aid the afflicted. We serve the poor and the downtrodden. We have malice towards none. Why should we be afraid?'

Alas! She did not realize that looters follow a different set of rules. They are an enemy of the good and a scourge to the virtuous. They are opposed to every civilized men and women of the world.

Mother Superior realized her mistake before long.

It was five in the afternoon. The snows of Pir Panjal was tinged with the pink of the setting sun. The shadows of the poplar trees had lengthened over the green grass bed. The tired Gujjar shepherds, in shabby long robes and caps, were homeward-bound with their sheep and chewing raw corn.

The closing bell of the convent school had been sounded long since. The students had already returned to their homes. In the hospital, the sick lay stretched on their beds. Just then, a commotion was heard. In the melee, a band of intruders barged into the convent.

A number of foreigners were staying in the guest house there. Some were new arrivals, while others were staying there for long. Colonel V.O.T. Dykes, an old Englishman, was one among them. Formerly of the Indian Air Force, he had stayed back in India after retirement. He lived here in the convent with his wife. Although crippled with arthritis, he did his best in helping the sisters with keeping the accounts every now and then. In this crisis, the old man came to the forefront, gun in hand, to stop the intruders outside the convent.

But old age had enfeebled Dykes and his eyesight was poor. Before he could aim the gun with his arthritic arms, he was felled by their bullet.

Mrs Dykes was right behind her husband, stricken with fear. The invaders pounced on her like a pack of wild animals on a scared rabbit. A wail was heard just once. It got drowned by the loud swagger and bluster of the invaders. Two days later, the unclad body of Mrs Dykes was found inside a deep well. Even the clothes of the dead woman were taken away by her killers.

The looters were expecting to take away sackfuls of valuables from the convent. But their hopes were dashed. A convent was meant to render service and not to hoard precious jewellery and stones. So they scrambled for the clock on the wall, clothes on the rack, and curtains on the windows.

The rage of the looters increased in proportion to the meagreness of the pillage. They vented their anger by breaking things – chairs, tables, almirahs, chest of drawers, crockery, glasses, doors, and windows. Even the white marble crosses over the graves in the garden outside were broken to pieces.

Their rage was not spent yet. On the contrary, they bayed for blood. They brought nine foreigner sisters of the convent at gunpoint and lined them up in the courtyard. Nine of the invaders aimed their rifles at their forehead, ready to press the trigger. Certain of the impending death, the sisters closed their eyes in silent prayer to God.

But who can harm the one whom Christ protects? The nine innocent sisters were saved by God, apparently over a trifling thing. One of the sisters had a gold tooth. Spotting it, one of the killers dropped his rifle and ran for it. But his fellow looters were equally hawk-eyed for the loot. So a quarrel started among them that soon snowballed into a fight over the bit of gold. In the middle of the ruckus, a headman arrived. He had the rectitude to understand that it was one thing to kill Kashmiri men and women, but quite another to kill European nuns. Thus, they were saved miraculously at the nick of time.

A separate band of intruders were busy in another part of the convent. They raided the hospital and broke anything they came across into pieces, and killed or wounded anyone who crossed their path. The costly X-ray machine was broken into pieces by the butt of their gun. Jars and bottles were crushed and the medicines in them were spilled; the sick and hapless men and women were bruised and hurt. In the end, a nurse was killed and two of the patients breathed their last.

Sister Teresalina, a pure soul and assistant Mother Superior of the convent, also lost her life. She came from far-off Spain to Baramulla with the vow of service. She had stationed herself at the door to the temple so as to prevent its desecration by the invaders. She took a bullet in her chest.

That day in Baramulla, a delicate sapling was vandalized by the invaders. The mellow light of the lamp was blown out on the altar of humanitarian service. The white marble plaque was stained by the blood of the innocent.

After tanking up on petrol at Srinagar, the Indian army finally arrived at Baramulla. By then, the sun had set and dusk descended gradually.

The town lay quiet and desolate. Baramulla resembled a wounded man, knocked unconscious by repeated blows, motionless and comatose. Its streets were deserted and the houses were empty. Corpses lay strewn by the roadside and on the courtyards. Vultures were feasting on them and stray dogs and jackals were fighting over the flesh. A sad spectacle; Baramulla used to be a town, but now it was a graveyard.

The very next morning, Brigadier Sen's troops went out in search of the invaders. But they were hard to come by, having fled quite far off. While fleeing, they had damaged the roads to deter the Indian army from pursuing them. Giant tree trunks were laid across the road. Elsewhere, big rocks were rolled down from the hillside. It was impossible for the jeeps and buses to advance without removing the obstacles. Moreover, fuel would run dry from time to time. They had to wait for petrol to arrive from Srinagar.

Thus, the Indian troops arrived at Rampur. The journey of a few hours took a few days.

The residents of Srinagar oscillated between hope and despair, unsure of what lay ahead. Selatong was round the corner, and the gunfight was within earshot. News travelled by word of mouth. But now, the enemy had been driven far off. Nobody knew about the outcome of the battle there. Rumours could hardly be verified. Morning brought the news of the Indian army having vanquished the invaders. Everybody heaved a sigh of relief. The very next moment, the inverse was heard. The invaders had crushed the Indian army and were advancing towards Srinagar. Faces turned pale with fear; heartbeats increased. People pondered over whether to pack and move. Days rolled by in this manner.

One evening, the lights of Srinagar dazzled all of a sudden.

Young and old, men and women stared blankly for a while. The initial surprise gave way to euphoria. Indian soldiers had indeed reached Mahura and had driven out the enemy. They embraced each other and shouted, 'Mahura is ours!'

It was true. Brigadier Sen's troops had reached Mahura from Rampur. These days, a number of engineers accompanied the army. They did not fight, but kept the equipment fighting fit. They were experts in hacking a dead machine alive. None could match their skills in fixing a jeep, lorry, motor car, or a tank. A hydroelectric plant might have been a new challenge to them, but never an impossible one. After a few days' tinkering, they brought the broken pieces together and the dynamo of the electricity plant was back in action. The capital city was lit up. And not just its streets and houses, but people's minds too.

The road from Mahura to Uri was lined by towering mountain ranges and dense forests. From this hideout, the enemy might launch an ambush at any moment. The Indian troops now had to proceed with caution. They had to take the help of the air force for reconnaissance.

Srinagar airport was small, having been built by the Maharaja for his personal aircraft. Those were small and light airplanes meant for pleasure trips. The runway was narrow, and air traffic control, air flow, and weather-measuring instruments were ordinary. It had no provision to handle large aircrafts. The top brass of the Indian air force then were almost all English. They arrived from Delhi and inspected the airport. The experts examined the length, breadth, and area for two whole days. Then the measurements were analysed threadbare and voluminous equations were worked out. Thereafter, a detailed report was drawn concluding that Srinagar airport was not fit for fighter aircrafts.

Expert opinion had to be obeyed. The aircrafts were compelled to fly to Srinagar all the way from Palam. It was disadvantageous. The already limited fuel in these aircrafts would get exhausted on the to-and-fro journey.

Within a few days, this problem was resolved by a miraculous incident.

There was a special arrangement so that the combat zone in the mountain and forest can be spotted from the air, without delay. On being prompted by the headquarters at Delhi, Indian troops would light a fire on the edges of their camp. The aircrafts could easily spot their positions.

That morning, two Spitfires took off from Palam with two young air force pilots. They flew to Pattan, but failed to spot any fire signal below. The radio operator had made some mistake in relaying the news. Hence, Brigadier Sen's office was unaware of the sortie from Delhi.

But what to do now? Should they fly back to Delhi? What alternative do they have? The pilots regretted aborting the mission after wasting so much fuel for nothing. One pilot gathered his thoughts and radioed the other, 'How about landing at the Srinagar airport to enquire?'

The second pilot replied, 'We might, but we have orders that Spitfires can't be landed here.'

The first pilot was confident, 'Whatever the bosses say, I can surely land my plane in that airstrip.'

The second one said, 'Me too.'

'Then let's go for it. Jai Hind!'

'Ready, one two, three ... ' and they swooped down.

One after the other, the two Spitfires landed safely on the small runway to the utter surprise of the airport officers and air traffic control. One wrong turn showed the right way. At the airport, the pilots marked the battlefront with red pencils on their maps. Then they took to air and, after firing upon enemy positions, returned to Delhi before evening.

What aeronautical science had considered impossible was made possible by two intrepid Indian youths. Their achievement inspired their comrades and filled the hearts of every Indian with pride.

The very next day, a new base was opened by the Indian Air Force at the Srinagar airport. Several Spitfires reached there from Delhi. Along came the crew, fitter, mechanic, ground engineer, pilot, officer, and other air force staff and their machinery and equipment. Group Captain Mehar Singh, DSO, arrived as the commander.

Brigadier Sen's troops left Mahura in search of the intruders with the aid of the air force. Small enemy detachments that were hiding in the nearby forests were gunned down by the Indian troops. But the main column was still far afield. Speedy pursuit was needed to catch up with them.

Advancing some more, they came to a big channel, wide and deep, through which a mountain stream was gushing past. Vehicles could not cross it. The stone viaduct over it had been blown off by the intruders.

The engineers were called. They said that building a bridge would need heavy equipment and sufficient time, both of which were in short supply.

But Brigadier Sen was undaunted under all circumstances. He said, 'Let the cars, jeeps, and trucks remain here. The enemy have to be pursued on foot. We must capture Uri by any means.'

The soldiers saluted, 'Yes, Sir.'

They chased the enemy on foot and captured Uri. Three weeks before on 11 November, at the very spot where Brigadier Rajendra Singh had laid down his life fighting the enemy, Brigadier L.P. Sen raised the tricoloured national flag of independent India for the first time. All joined their voices to shout 'Jai Hind', the rallying cry of independent India.

The army band played, 'Jana Gana Mana Adhinayaka – ' The national anthem of independent India was heard for the first time in Uri.

Before the celebrations faded in Uri, ominous news arrived. This time, it was from Jammu.

With Jammu and Ladakh on either sides and Kashmir in the middle, the three provinces constituted the state of Maharaja Hari Singh. Big cities and military cantonments of West Pakistan like Sialkot, Wazirabad, and Mari lay across the border from Jammu. The intruders had launched the attack from there. They had already captured a large area, besides perpetrating the usual murder, loot, and injury.

The intruders in Kashmir were all outsiders. It was easy to resist them. But the intruders in Jammu were joined by some local Muslims. Such traitors were the most dangerous. Sardar Ibrahim Khan was their leader. Maharaja Hari Singh had a feudatory lord in Poonch, who had the title of raja. He was both valiant and benevolent as befits a king. Ibrahim was his subject. Noticing his brilliance, the raja took the boy under his wings and saw him through school, college, and further education in Britain. Ibrahim returned home a barrister due to the munificence of the raja. Educated Muslims were hard to come by in Jammu. The new barrister became their leader in no time.

By that time, the Muslim League had become influential in Punjab. Riding on the wave of communalism and Hindu hatred, they had floated the ship of two-nation theory. That rang certain bells in Ibrahim's clever head. Like other opportunists, he came aboard the ship with many of his camp followers. He started conspiring against the king whose generosity had brought him this far. There were very few examples of such crass ungratefulness in history.

As traitors are never short of trickery and criminals their accomplices, Ibrahim Khan found his partner in crime in Abdul Qayyum Khan, the prime minister of North-West Frontier Province. He too had a fascinating record of changing colours.

Qayyum had started off as a nationalist Muslim. He had his seat beside the Congress leader Bhulabhai Desai in the front row of the central legislature in Delhi. A bitter critic of the English, he termed communalism as poison. His picture figured in the album of national leaders and he delivered speeches at nationalist gatherings.

Suddenly, he changed his mind and direction and joined the Muslim League. Overnight, he started abusing the Congress. Gandhi to him was an imposter, Nehru was obdurate, and Patel? He was a devil incarnate, the foremost enemy of the Muslims.

The Congress leaders were locked up, at the time, in the house of Aga Khan at Ahmednagar. They were astounded by the antics of their old comrade and wondered what a calamity it was!

It is said that no one makes for the bitterest enemies but one's own people. It appeared that Abdul Qayyum Khan's greatest indignation was reserved for India. The planning and execution of the invasion of Kashmir was done from Peshawar and Qayyum was one of its masterminds. Sardar Ibrahim Khan was in constant touch with him. After gathering arms and men, he revolted against the raja, saying, 'Raja and Maharaja be damned. We have formed a new state, its name is Azad Kashmir.'

Maharaja Hari Singh's army camps were at Mirpur, Poonch, Naushera, and Rajouri. But they were inadequately manned and armed. On top of that, they were overcrowded by the Hindu and Sikh refugees fleeing from Pakistan. A mass of tired, wounded, and bereft men and women. It was difficult to provide food and shelter to them. The invaders were surrounding these camps.

Hearing this news, the Indian government despatched troops towards Poonch.

But there was hardly any road there. It was just a walking trail meandering through dense forests. After following that trail and crossing the eight thousand feet high Haji Pir Pass with great difficulty, the battalion of Brigadier Pritam Singh finally reached the army camp at Poonch.

Food was in short supply there. Thousands of invaders were preying upon the town like a predator from all sides. It was impossible to avert their gaze and bring supplies from outside. The food stocked in the homes and at the depots had almost run out. The only way to bring food grains from outside was by air. But where would the plane land? The troops at the camps were trying their best to keep the invaders at bay. Who would build the runway? Pritam Singh was all at sea.

There was a Hindu carpenter among the refugees in Poonch. One day, he arrived at the office of Pritam Singh, wishing to meet the brigadier. His orderlies tried to shoo him away, but they relented after a lot of coaxing and cajoling from the man. So they took him to meet Pritam Singh.

The old man saluted him and said, 'Sir, engage me in your work.'

Brigadier Singh asked, 'You are an old man, what can you do?'

The old man replied, 'Can prepare the ground for aircrafts.'

Pritam Singh was surprised, 'Runway? What do you know of it?'

The old man said, 'Sir, I know nothing other than hard work. Your engineers will draw the plan, the masons will do the brick work, and I will carry the soil, water, lime, moraine, and cement.'

Pritam Singh was unconvinced, 'Come on. Your weak frame cannot possibly withstand such hard labour.'

The old man's eyes moistened. Touching his forehead with his hands, he said, 'My lord, these hardened bones have suffered a lot. My two young sons died at the hands of the intruders and my only daughter is still untraced. I have walked for fifteen kilometres in the dead of night, holding the hand of my sick wife. How long will I live and for what? If I can do my bit in building the airport, then I will die in peace.'

The old man could not be placated by any means.

Next morning, Pritam Singh woke up to the din of a crowd. Looking out of the window, he saw about two thousand refugees, old and young, men and women. Each one of them wanted to lend a hand in building the airport. They said, 'If the old carpenter can carry load, then we too can.'

The work to build the runway started with great fervour. The trees and bushes were cleared and the ground was levelled. Brick, lime, and moraine were laid for the take-off and landing of aircrafts. Even the weak and the infirm did their bit. They looked after the households and the children of those who went out to work. A month's job was completed in a week. Provisions were flown in for the blockaded inhabitants of Poonch.

The invaders had thought that the people in the camps would recapitulate in a matter of days due to starvation. That eventuality was obviated. After a lot of deliberations, they brought in an imported 3.7 howitzer. They fired shells from atop the mountains that kept landing right on the runway. The flight operations had to be stopped.

Food scarcity returned to the town. Stocks were made to last for a few more days through rationing. The army reduced their quota so as to feed the children. But for how long?

Pritam Singh called the signal corps and said, 'Enough is enough! The enemy cannon on the mountain has to be silenced.

Wire the headquarters to send a couple of long-range guns here and leave the rest to us.'

That was easier said than done. Still the HQ honchos said, 'No harm in trying?'

One afternoon, three air force Dakotas took off with a few 20 pounder cannons, ammunition, and artillery men. Air Commodore Mehar Singh, the head of the air force in Kashmir, thought the better of leaving this dangerous mission to the pilots alone. His army counterpart General Kulwant Singh, was of the same opinion. So the two of them hopped on to a Howard aircraft.

Within a short time, the four aircraft reached Poonch. Just as the first Dakota was about to land, the enemy howitzer on the mountain opened firing with a deep rumble. A shell burst like a thunderclap very close to the Dakota. The right wing of the aircraft was saved by a whisker. Mehar Singh realized that the attempt was futile. Landing an aircraft under such conditions was akin to suicide. He radioed the order for all the aircraft to return to base. The refugees at the Poonch camp sighed in despondency. A loud cheer went up at the enemy camp on the mountain.

Mehar Singh was never short on ideas. In the evening, he called his handpicked pilots and said, 'Friends, what cannot be done by hook has to be done by crook. We will have to outwit the enemy to accomplish the task.'

He disclosed his plans. The pilots were pleased to hear that. Novelty excites these young fellows and danger makes them even more desperate.

In Poonch, evening had set in for quite some time. A waxing half-moon adorned the sky. In the half-light, the distant sal forest and paddy fields appeared to be wrapped in mist. A quiet tranquillity had permeated the water, land, and sky, as if drowsiness had enveloped mother nature.

Suddenly, the calmness was rudely broken by a thunderclap. No, not from the cloud, but from fighter planes. Twenty of them had reached Poonch, with Mehar Singh himself piloting the first of them.

The invaders hurriedly loaded the shells into the cannon. But the planes were just circling the sky and not landing on the ground. This perplexed the invaders. The planes could not be seen, nor their numbers be ascertained.

In this twilight zone of confusion and darkness, one of the Dakotas suddenly dived below and landed. Pritam Singh's men were ready at the aerodrome. They quickly emptied the plane of its cargo. Within a few minutes, it took to air and joined the fleet hovering overhead. None could notice the manoeuvre in the midst of the flight of the planes and their collective roar.

One by one, the Dakotas landed, emptied the equipment, and returned to the sky to join the rest, all without alerting the enemy. Within half an hour, Mehar Singh returned with his fleet to his base like a victor.

The enemy on the mountain were also happy in the belief that the Indian planes did not dare land in Poonch. They had a hearty laugh thinking that the infidels had fled out of fear.

But their amusement was short-lived. No sooner had dawn broken than the twenty pounders started shelling from the camp at Poonch. Their range, firepower, and sound were in a class of their own. The intruders ran for dear life, leaving their guns and equipment behind.

Poonch was saved but not liberated. The fort was strengthened but not freed. The enemy had already entrenched itself at Naushera and the adjoining villages and had also positioned itself on the mountain top. They were like drawbridges to Poonch. Unless they were dislodged from those positions, it would be difficult to free Poonch.

When the going gets tough, the tough gets going. That was the motto of Brigadier Usman. He had arrived at Jhangarh near Naushera, as the commander of the 50th Parachute Brigade. The invaders had launched a fierce attack there with mortars and machine guns. The Indian army was hard put to resist them.

Usman hailed from Azamgarh district of Uttar Pradesh. After matriculation from Harish Chandra College in Benaras and BA from Allahabad University, he went to Britain to study warfare. He was the last Indian student at Sandhurst.

From a young age, Usman possessed an unusual degree of fortitude. He seemed to be wrought from a class of iron that could be broken but not bent. His other possession was deep patriotism. At a banquet in Britain, a sectarian Muslim leader occupied the chair to the right of Usman. Coming to know his name, the leader said in a patronizing tone, 'So you belong to the Muslim nation? Me too. Pleased to …'

Usman stopped him midway and said, 'My nationality is Indian. But if you ask my religion, then yes, it's Islam.'

The leader was left speechless. He also lost his appetite for the food in front of him.

At the time of partition, Usman was serving in Multan in West Punjab. He had witnessed many instances of communal barbarism and had personally saved many hapless Hindus and Sikhs. That had an impact on his life thereafter. From the day after Gandhi's assassination, Usman stopped eating fish and meat and had turned a vegetarian.

Two days after Brigadier Usman arrived in Jhangarh as commander, the Indian soldiers suffered a defeat. They had to retreat several miles. A lesser man would have been dejected from this initial setback. But Usman became more determined. He started planning a counter-attack. Through tireless efforts, he stocked up on arms, ammunition, and provisions. He raised a civilian volunteer force with the local youth and perfected the communication signal system. He shored up the morale and confidence of his brother officers and soldiers.

Usman first snatched Kot from the invaders. Though a small village hamlet, Kot had immense strategic importance. The road from Naushera, Jhangarh, Rajouri, and Poonch converged at this place.

After Kot, Naushera was occupied.

The enemy headquarters was alarmed at the developments. The chiefs in their anger sacked the leader of Kot, while the commander of Naushera was thrown into prison. A new commander was sent to war at the head of thousands of soldiers. The order was to reoccupy the lost ground. Defeat and desertion will attract the death penalty. Either Naushera or death.

Out of desperation, the invaders attacked Naushera in the dead of night. The attack was carried out on three fronts on the east, south, and the north by almost fifteen thousand invaders. They were carrying imported rifles, medium and light machine guns, mortars, and grenades. The modern tactical manoeuvre displayed in the attack left no room for doubt as to who the masterminds were behind the war and the invasion of Kashmir.

The soldiers of the para brigade valiantly resisted this huge surge of the enemy. The mission of the invaders was to capture Naushera at any cost. The vow of the Indian soldiers was to protect Naushera at all costs. Such a fierce battle was not witnessed in the Kashmir conflict. Each side had pledged their life on it.

Brigadier Usman commanded his soldiers from the front. Wherever he sensed any danger, he moved there.

Night ended in morning, morning rolled onto afternoon, and the tired afternoon sun finally went down; but the grim battle and the killings wore on.

The invaders scored not in bravery, but in numbers. One dead soldier was replaced by eleven more. This superiority in numbers made the Indian soldiers vulnerable. The enemy advanced to within fifty gauge and gradually even nearer.

Brigadier Usman had realized from the outset that the enemy were innumerable, four times his own numbers. He had asked for help from the nearest camp. While commanding his soldiers, he counted the minutes, wondering when the reinforcements would arrive and whether his army could hold out against the enemy and thwart its advance.

Usman looked at his watch time and again. It was a race between him and his soldiers against the hands of the clock. Chances of victory receded with every passing minute.

Eventually, the enemy advanced even closer, almost breathing down their neck. Usman looked restlessly to his left, right, and back. Soldiers, even more soldiers were needed right now. But where were they? Looking at the army camp, he saw some engineers repairing equipment at the workshop. The brigadier shouted out, 'Every hand to the front with guns. Stop the enemy by any means.'

The engineers dropped their hammers and picked up weapons. The supplies people, who usually worked far behind the battlefront, joined the fight too.

The brigadier was making a whirlwind tour of the camps. Anybody whom he came across was despatched to the battlefront. 'Who are you? The cook? Leave it for later. Now go and fight. You are a kitchen help? Doesn't matter. Go and stop the invaders.' The one who had kept the accounts all his life had to put down his pen and pick up the gun.

'Sat Sri Akaal!'

The battle cry of the Sikh soldiers was heard from behind. Reinforcements had arrived at long last. Five more minutes, and Usman's soldiers would have been wiped out. The worst was over now. It was really a close call.

Along with the fresh soldiers arrived a few fighter planes of the Indian Air Force. The invaders could hardly withstand the ground attack by the Sikh soldiers and firing from air by the fighter planes.

Bodies of the dead invaders in their thousands littered the fields, roads, mountainside, and everywhere else. Shouts of the victorious Indian soldiers reverberated through the valley. The battle for Naushera ended. The invaders were decimated.

A new campaign commenced, this time from Naushera to Jhangarh. The route lay through the Gaikot forest. The Indian army had to advance cautiously so as to avoid the enemy. They had to hide behind bushes, run, walk, and crawl on all fours, or even move on their chests.

Usman reached the base of the mountain with his army, quiet like a wolf stalking its prey. They took positions behind the tall trees.

The invaders had entrenched themselves on this mountain for quite some time. Light and medium machine guns were positioned on the peaks. The whole area was cordoned off with wire fencing. The path to the mountaintop was guarded by armed personnel.

As the daylight faded from the western horizon, darkness engulfed the treetops, and the crickets started their collective chirping, suddenly an Indian sepoy jumped from the treetop on to the shoulder of the first guardsman. He was choked to death with an iron grip before he could make any sound. The second guardsman stood some distance away. Another sepoy sneaked up from behind and planted a shining knife on his back. A muffled groan was heard, and then all was still and quite. The wretched fellow could not even utter the name of Allah.

The rest of the soldiers then came out of hiding, as if emerging from the rocks by magic. The invaders were not at all prepared for this sudden attack. After a bit of resistance, they fled. On capturing the camp, the Indian soldiers found that they had left behind not just arms and ammunitions, but clothes and shoes too. The kitchen contained stacks of hot chapattis, a pitcher full of liquor, and a container full of goat meat. In their tearing hurry to flee, the food was left untouched.

The flagpole of Jhangarh once again sported the Indian tricolour. That night, the entire army rank and file sat down for a feast in the illumination of the gaslights. It was accompanied by song, dance, and music celebrating the victory. After two months and twenty-five days, a bed was prepared for Brigadier Usman. Like Rana Pratap, he too had pledged to sleep on the floor till Jhangarh was wrested from the enemy.

Naushera and Jhangarh were like two columns of a gateway. Losing them had put the enemy in trouble. The supply lines of

Pakistan fell within the range of Indian guns, an easy target for the gunners. Like the ace of spades, whoever controls Jhangarh wins. That's why the invaders kept on shelling Jhangarh from afar, time and again.

It was the fourth of July. The enemy started shelling Jhangarh at night. Shells kept on falling indiscriminately and from all directions on the camp. Streaks of fire criss-crossed the night sky as if it was Diwali.

Brigadier Usman was always by the side of his soldiers at all moments of crisis. That night too, he was fleeting from one bunker to the other in the hailstorm of fire, enquiring after his men. Suddenly, a shell burst very close to him.

The doctor and support staff at the camp tried their best. They can only give medicines, not life. As the night faded and the stars too, and the moon went down behind the hills, Brigadier Usman breathed his last and mingled with the gentle morning breeze. At the Jhangarh camp, the eyes of the battle-hardened soldiers were moistened too. As the news reached Pakistan, they rose in celebration. It was Diwali at the invaders camp at Peshawar.

The mortal remains of the brave soldier was decked with flowers and flown down to New Delhi. There, the Hindus, Sikhs, Christians, Parsis, and Muslims paid their last respects with flowers. His coffin was draped with the national flag and borne on a gun carriage with full state honours. It was accompanied by the chiefs of the army, navy, and air force, other generals, as well as the entire cabinet and Prime Minister Nehru himself. Thousands of men and women from all communities lined the street to pay their last respects.

Independent India had not witnessed such a universal outpouring of grief since the death of Mahatma Gandhi, nor such an outpouring of respect.

The victorious march of the Indian army rolled on gradually. It trampled upon the yearnings of the invaders and the conspiracy and wishfulness of Pakistan. Kashmir valley and the enemy-controlled areas around Jammu were liberated. The misadventure of capturing Kashmir by force failed. The dream of raising the Pakistani flag atop Raj Bhavan in Srinagar was never fulfilled.

In time, normalcy returned to Kashmir. Trade and commerce commenced, classes began to be held in schools and colleges, work started in offices and courts. Caddies with their golf bags and old golfers in their finery reappeared on the soft, green fairways of Gulmarg. Adventurous girls and boys rode the ponies to Khilanmarg to ski down the icy slopes. The houseboats on the Jhelum started lifting their shutters one by one. The hawkers rowed their shikaras, laden with woodwork, papier mâché containers, and embroidered shawls to the doors of the foreign tourists.

The danger had lifted from the capital. But the days of the monarchy became numbered. Maharaja Hari Singh's throne had become untenable.

Fairy tale princes become kings, sons of nobles inherit the office, and sons of merchants ride the waves to faraway lands for commerce.

The regent of Kashmir, Hari Singh was not the king's son, but his nephew. The old Maharaja Pratap Singh was Hari Singh's uncle. Without a son, the king had left the kingdom to his nephew prior to his death. That had raised quite a few eyebrows.

And that was in order. Hari Singh's father Amar Singh was Maharaja Pratap Singh's own brother. They were suckled by the same mother, played with each other, and went to sleep hearing the same fairy tale from the matron. As boys, they were taught by the same teacher and went for hunting together in their youth. Once they reached adulthood, they fell apart on the question of succession to the throne. Amar Singh conspired to remove Pratap Singh and become the king. To know that story, one has to look far into the past and browse through the dusty old pages of history.

Almost a hundred years ago, Punjab *kesari* (lion) Ranjit Singh was the suzerain of the Sikh empire. He had a young commander in his army, the Dogra Rajput Gulab Singh. He was as brave as he was clever. Pleased with him, Maharaja Ranjit bestowed upon him the province of Jammu. Commander Gulab Singh became Raja Gulab Singh.

The boundaries of the Jammu province gradually increased. Gulab Singh added Baltistan and conquered Ladakh. His sword and his intelligence were equally sharp. It did not take long for him to understand that the days of the Mughal empire was numbered, that the Sikh empire was in its last throes, and the English were the future suzerain of India. By that time, Ranjit Singh had breathed his last in Lahore.

Fortune favours the brave. Beleaguered by the frontier wars, the English sought Gulab Singh's help. The raja lavishly bestowed money, food, and shelter to the English army. Four years later, the English troops defeated the Sikh army and occupied Lahore. By the Treaty of Amritsar, Gulab Singh got the rights to the mountainous regions adjoining Jammu against payment of two crore rupees. His kingdom now extended from the east of river Sindh to the west of river Ravi, including Kashmir and Gilgit.

Gulab Singh got the rights to the new territories but not their occupancy. The ruler of Kashmir Sheikh Imamuddin would not allow anyone to step on his territory. In the end, troops marched from Jammu and defeated Imamuddin. Maharaja Gulab Singh occupied the throne of Kashmir.

After Gulab Singh's death, his son Ranbir Singh became the king. He continued the policies of his father in helping the

British in every manner. During the sepoy mutiny, he had sent his troops to save many an English life.

It was not in the nature of the English to remember its benefactors. When the storm had blown over, the English forgot the help rendered by the Dogra dynasty. The British rulers had realized the strategic importance of Kashmir. They understood that an English army base was necessary in Gilgit to stave off the Afghan, Chinese, and Tzarist Russia. They agonized over their own folly of having bartered away their interests in Kashmir.

Then they started plotting so as to perpetuate English domination in Kashmir through various artifices.

Ranbir Singh's eldest son Pratap Singh was a harmless person, more inclined to spend his time in prayer, meditation, and worship.

Finding the time propitious, the English installed a residency in Kashmir, another name for the Big Brother office. Sir Oliver Saint John arrived as its head – the first Resident of Kashmir.

Once allowed a toehold, the English Resident, like the proverbial camel, knew how to occupy the whole room. It was even more so with the Resident Plowden, who was as cunning as he was unscrupulous. He brought the men in the king's court around to his side either through bribery or through fear. Even the Maharaja's revenue minister secretly joined the cabal.

One morning, as Maharaja Pratap Singh sat down for his rituals, his younger brother Amar Singh came and said, 'Brother, come outside. I need to talk urgently.'

One could not leave the prayer mat without completing the ritual. The Maharaja indicated so to his brother.

Amar Singh raised his voice further, 'To hell with your rituals! Save your kingdom first and then sit down for your religious rituals. If you can save your own head, come and pour holy water on your deity's head.'

The Maharaja came out of the temple in anxiety and asked, 'What is the matter?'

Amar Singh replied, 'Not here, let's go to your bedroom.' After closing the doors and windows cautiously, Amar Singh disclosed the grave news under his breath.

The English Resident had intercepted several secret missives. All were written under the hand of Maharaja Pratap Singh. He was conspiring with the Russians against the English. The Maharaja was secretly plotting to kill Resident Plowden.

As he heard that, tears rolled down his cheeks. He said, 'This is sheer conspiracy to dethrone me by spreading calumny against my name.'

Amar Singh was unconvinced, 'Conspiracy?'

Maharaja said, 'Yes, and you are part of the conspiracy.' He held his younger brother's hand and beseeched, 'My brother, I know that you long to occupy the throne of Kashmir. But God will not forgive that which you are doing. Relent.'

Amar Singh muttered haltingly, 'Me … and … conspiracy, how come … ?' Unable to proceed further, he quickly withdrew from the Maharaja's presence.

It did not take long for the Maharaja to understand that Resident Plowden and his brother Amar Singh had spread a dragnet all around him. He was in mortal danger. But not knowing the way out of the quagmire, he fidgeted helplessly like a trapped animal. Finally, he told the Maharani, 'When my own brother has become my adversary, what's the use of seeking salvation? I leave it to my fate.'

Since that day, Pratap Singh stopped taking any food or drink.

The Resident drew an order, stating that the Maharaja had voluntarily abdicated his throne. It also asked the Government of India to make arrangements for good governance without delay.

At first, the Maharaja refused to sign the letter. But Amar Singh intimidated him relentlessly. After three days of fasting, an enfeebled Pratap Singh finally signed away his own order of dismissal.

The governance of the province was taken over by a new council of ministers. Raja Amar Singh became its de jure president. But Resident Plowden remained its de facto head. The English built a fort at Gilgit, with cannons, guns, and a British regiment firmly in place.

The hapless and deposed Maharaja Pratap Singh was relegated, like a prisoner, to a corner of his own palace in his own kingdom. The forlorn and unhappy days stretched endlessly before him. The months and years dragged on interminably. Then, out of desperation, the Maharaja wrote a letter himself to the viceroy Lord Lansdowne. The drafting of the letter was amateurish and its wording imprecise, but its meaning was clear and earnest. He stated that the story of his collusion with the Russians was false. The letters that were cited by the Resident were fabricated. Hence, either the Maharaja be restored his throne or he be shot on his chest and killed. He is unable to bear such a wretched existence any longer.

All of a sudden, an exact copy of a government document was published in a newspaper from Kolkata. It revealed the English machinations in Kashmir and the subterfuge employed by the resident Plowden. The Parliament was rocked. Charles Bradlow, a liberal member, took the side of the Maharaja. William Digby, one of the righteous Englishmen of the times, strongly denounced the injustice meted out to the Maharaja. The Government of India was obliged to restore his dominion. Maharaja Pratap Singh reoccupied the throne of Kashmir after fifteen years. He lived for another twenty years. Amar Singh predeceased him and Hari Singh joined the Maharaja's council of ministers.

Pratap Singh's queen remarked, 'I will adopt a son, but under no circumstances shall I allow the son of the traitor to ascend the throne.' But Pratap Singh kept quiet. None could read his mind.

In time, age caught up with the Maharaja. He was stricken by various ailments of old age and was confined to his bed. His personal physician routinely paid visits twice a day and recommended various pills and concoctions, but to no avail.

The Maharaja did not recover. Pratap Singh realized that his time was up. He called up his friends, nobles, and advisors and, touching the head of his nephew Hari Singh, he proclaimed, 'Let it be known that he is my successor, the future king of Jammu & Kashmir.'

The Maharani was sitting beside her husband. She said between her sobs, 'Maharaja, what have you done? Ultimately, you gave away your kingdom to Amar Singh's son?' But no reply came as, by that time, Pratap Singh had closed his eyes. They were not to be opened ever again.

After ascending the throne, Maharaja Hari Singh turned his attention to the welfare of his subjects. He enacted laws to bar foreigners from taking over plum posts in the kingdom and kept a watchful eye over his servants so that they do not sleep on their jobs. He toured the villages to personally see the condition of the peasants. He went out in his shikara in person to rescue men and women afflicted by the flooding of the Jhelum River. At the round table conference in Britain, he spoke in favour of self-rule by the Indians. Such opinion had seldom been heard from a native Indian ruler before.

The English rulers were not amused. They were unhappy for not having complete control over Kashmir. Now they became positively angry, and tried to foment trouble in Kashmir.

It could be easily accomplished. Kashmiri subjects were unlettered Muslims. It did not take much to ignite communal passions. An Englishman named Wakefield was there in

Maharaja Hari Singh's council of ministers, through whom the Muslims of Jammu & Kashmir were incited. Fuel was added to the flame of discontent from outside the state. Fundamentalist Muslim groups like the Ahrars and Ahmadis of Punjab and their Urdu newspapers decried that the Hindu Maharaja and his officials were torturing the Muslims.

The *Siasat Daily* in Lahore openly appealed to the Muslims to pledge their lives in the name of Allah. Let them kill the enemy and uproot the government of the infidels. Thousands of free copies of the daily were distributed in Srinagar, Sopore, Bijbehera, and other towns. Underground magazines like *Kashmir Majlis* and *Maktabi Kashmir* were widely circulated in the markets, meetings, and masjids, and among the madrasa students in remote villages. Numerous copies arrived either by post or by hand. They were printed in red ink and dripped with violence, which would arouse murderous instincts even in a gentle person.

The movement within the state was led by a young and educated Muslim youth named Sheikh Abdullah.

Sheikh Abdullah was born in an ordinary Kashmiri family. His father wove woollen shawls and his mother, besides tending to the household, used to prepare pressed rice to sell in the market. After completing school education, he went to college in Lahore and then to Aligarh.

In India, the British had sown the seeds of Hindu-Muslim enmity. And its ground was prepared at Aligarh. The English vice chancellor of the Aligarh Muslim University, Mr Beck, and Prof. Theodore Morrison had supplied the soil, fertilizer, and water. They had nurtured the sapling of communal violence. Under official patronage and encouragement, it had grown up to a giant poison tree, covered with thorns. One who had taken lessons under its shade, walked on the grass underneath, and breathed the air around could hardly be expected to be a lover incarnate. Water lilies do not bloom in the desert. It was no wonder that the student of Aligarh Muslim University, Sheikh Abdullah, would return to Kashmir and instigate the Muslims against the Hindus.

To begin with, he established a Muslim library in Fatekdal. Discontent against the government spread among the students there who arrived for study each evening. At the large Friday prayer gathering at Shah Hamdan Mosque, he would deliver inflammatory speeches. The witless Muslim folks were easily swayed by the mullahs. Clever Abdullah drew the chief Mirwaiz Maulana Yusuf Shah to his side. Bearing his religious decrees, Abdullah travelled from village to village to build up his support base.

Many among the state officials were foolhardy, whose insolence further intensified the agitation of the Muslim masses.

Such was the prevailing situation when Hari Singh lost his mind. There is a Christian saying that 'those whom the gods wish to destroy, they first make mad'. Instead of ruling his kingdom, the Maharaja abandoned himself to pleasure trips. Forgetting his royal duties and the upliftment of his subjects, he spent his time in London, Paris, and the Riviera. His cavorting there sometimes reached scandalous proportions. His extravagance quickly depleted the royal treasury. The residue left behind was usurped by the bureaucracy. Then they drew the noose tighter around the neck of the poor taxpayers to shore up the revenue.

And the reaction was not late in coming. The debacle occurred over a trivial incident. A small spark on an ammunition dump is enough for a big explosion.

It was mid-May of 1931. A Muslim policeman had not arrived for duty at the Jammu barracks. His senior Labhram was a Hindu Pandit from Kashmir. He came to enquire, only to find him fast asleep on his bed. Before the errant policeman could be chastised, he started abusing Labhram. Furious with rage, Labhram seized the mattress on his bed and dumped it on the floor of the room. A few pages of the holy Koran kept under the pillow were splayed on the floor.

How dare an infidel put his hands on the holy Koran and desecrate it? Abdullah and his team at the Fatekdal library roared in anger. They ensured that the news reached each and every Muslim in Jammu & Kashmir. Fuel was added to an already simmering discontent.

The government realized the seriousness of the situation. A member of the cabinet was entrusted with the enquiry. Evidence pointed to the innocence of Labhram. He was unaware that the holy book was there under the pillow. But to placate the Muslim community, Labhram was retired from service. The Muslim policeman too was dismissed from service for insubordination.

But the Muslim sentiment was not appeased. Sheikh Abdullah called for a meeting at the Khanqah-e-Moula in Srinagar. There a Pathan named Abdul Kader delivered a vitriolic speech against the Hindu Maharaja and his Hindu officials and subjects in front of thousands of inflamed Muslims. That man was a cook, newly arrived in Srinagar with his English master. The government arrested him on the charge of communalism.

On 13 July, Abdul Kader was to be tried at the Srinagar Central Jail. From early morning, people started gathering at the jail gate. They arrived in small and large processions from different regions. They hailed the martyr Abdul Kader and their intermittent uproar rattled the doors and windows of the jail.

Ultimately, the agitating mob spilled into the courtyard of the jail like floodwaters. The district magistrate and his officials showed utter lack of judgment. Without making any attempt to pacify the crowd, they fired on them resulting in the death of ten people and an equal number were injured.

All hell broke loose. A massive procession of people carried the dead bodies to the burial ground. The leaders from the library led a strong crowd of ten thousand. They carried a flag made from the blood-smeared clothes of the victims and shouted the worst about the Maharaja. It was more of a molten lava flow from a volcanic eruption than a procession.

The moving mass wound down the main avenue and reached Maharajganj Bazar. It was the largest business district of the capital. In a flash, the irate mob started attacking the Hindu men and women passers-by. Fierce rioting started in Srinagar that spread quickly to Vicharnag and other areas of the city. Hindu shops and businesses were looted and their houses were burnt down. Three were killed and one hundred sixty-three injured. The rioters vandalized the police stations and the telephone lines were snapped.

Wakefield was the dewan of Kashmir. He became incommunicado during the riot. The telephone in his bungalow rang continuously. Terrified Hindus were pleading for help to save their life and property; police, magistrates, and government officials were seeking directions. Wakefield's servant answered the calls with the same words, 'Sahib is not at home.'

When will he return?

He was clueless, 'Don't know, Sir.'

In the end, the Maharaja's troops were called from the barracks, which resorted to firing to quell the rioting and restored normalcy to the city.

The dewan reappeared late in the night and feigned ignorance about the happenings. 'What, riot! How dare? I'll teach a lesson to the scoundrels. I will throw them in jail, I'll hang them … ' Wakefield continued with his nonsense.

The Maharaja saw through the contrivance. Abdullah and his cohorts were arrested and put behind bars on Hari Parbat. Wakefield was thrown out and a host of worthless officials were removed from service. Communal stirrings were put down with an iron hand. That put an end to the British plan to dislodge the Maharaja on the plea of disturbance and assume control over Kashmir.

Fast forward to the future. Sheikh Abdullah had gone to Peshawar where he saw a huge public gathering of a hundred thousand people. Strapping Pathans were listening intently to a speech. Abdullah drew near out of curiosity.

On the stage was a trim man of medium height, long-nosed, fair-skinned, and wearing a white khadi cap. His broad forehead radiated intelligence, eyes burnt with the fire of courage, and the firm jaw hinted of determination. His voice lacked intensity but had firmness, just like a shining steel sword. Who was the man?

The speaker was none other than the Congress leader Pandit Jawaharlal Nehru. After the meeting was over, the listeners loudly hailed Nehru and surrounded him from all sides like devotees.

Sheikh Abdullah was taken by surprise. How could Nehru, a Hindu, win the heart and minds of the Muslim Pathans? What's the secret behind his appeal? He went to Nehru several times and spoke and listened to him at length. He learnt about the history of India's freedom movement and about the struggles of the Congress party.

Abdullah apprised Nehru of the pitiable condition of the Muslim peasants of Kashmir and how the Hindu Maharaja was exploiting them.

Nehru said that the peasants' misery was due to their poverty and not because they were Muslims. The rulers were heartless not because they were Hindus, but because they were autocratic.

It was a revelation for Abdullah.

Another incident happened on his way back from Peshawar. He was passing through an apple orchard. The Muslim owner was overseeing the harvesting of apples by his Hindu workers. He watched keenly so that no apple remained unplucked. The owner pushed the workers to climb higher up the tree. The branches drooped under their weight, and Abdullah feared that it would snap. Surely enough, a slender top branch broke and a twenty-year-old boy fell to the ground with a thud.

The owner came rushing and rained a number of blows with his stick. He added insult to injury by shouting, 'You idiot, you have broken a productive branch! Oh, such a loss! You will have to pay for it with your wages. Even that won't suffice.' And so he continued.

Abdullah and others lifted the injured and unconscious worker from the ground and took him to his home. There he saw the same poverty and distress that he had been witnessing in the dwellings of the Muslim artisans. He remembered the words of Nehru – the root cause of the people's distress is not religion but resources.

Abdullah's worldview changed and with it, his opinions. Indeed, he himself changed, as if being reborn.

Once again, some dispute erupted in the city between the Hindus and Muslims. It gradually snowballed into brickbats between the two parties. The Hindus were in greater danger, being smaller in number. For every Hindu household, there were ten Muslim households around. A Hindu girl had died of fever near Jhelum bridge number two. Her last rites were not performed for two days out of fear. The Hindus were not coming out of their homes even to buy provisions, let alone going to the burning ghat. Nobody wanted to lose their life in order to cremate the dead. The bereft mother was crying her heart out, clutching her dead girl.

Abdullah got the news and went to that house. He picked the little girl up in his own arms and rowed his shikara down the Jhelum to the cremation ground. Hundreds of Muslims followed the shikara on both banks of the Jhelum. They kept on deriding him, 'Shame, shame! Abdullah is taking the corpse of a kafir for cremation. The sheikh has turned an undertaker.'

Abdullah barked out, 'Nonsense! The dead has no religion, you fools.'

From then on, Abdullah became a new man. He built a new organization with members from all communities. Muslim Conference gave way to National Conference. The grand old Sikh Sardar Budh Singh became its president, the young Brahmin Prem Nath Bazaz its leader, and the Muslim Sheikh Abdullah its captain.

A mass movement of the people started in Kashmir. One who had been a Muslim leader for so long became the people's leader. Hindus and Muslims joined their voices to hail him, 'Sher-i-Kashmir zindabad!' He brought a ray of sunlight into the hutments of the ignorant, the blind, and the helpless men and women of Kashmir. To the deprived and dispossessed masses, he gave assurance and hope, a guideline for the present and a dream for the future.

Ram Chandra Kak became the prime minister of Maharaja Hari Singh at an unpropitious time. The man was a Kashmiri Pandit and was very shrewd. He had started off as a clerk in the library of Pratap Singh College in Srinagar, drawing a salary of rupees twenty. From there, he gradually rose to be the head of different departments, member of the legislature, minister in the cabinet, and finally the dewan to the Maharaja. He was adept as an administrator, but lacked political foresight. He made Congress a perpetual foe of the Maharaja. On his orders, Pandit Nehru was arrested in Kashmir, thereby creating a permanent chasm between the Maharaja of Kashmir and the future prime minister of India.

Misfortune never comes alone. A sanyasi by the name of Swami Santdev was spotted on the streets of Srinagar. Some say that he was two hundred years old, others vouch for five hundred. So long he had been meditating in the caves of the Himalayas. His disciples declared him to be an enlightened soul who can see the past as well as the future. By merely looking at one's face, he could relate the stories of previous and future births.

In time, his fame reached the Maharaja's ears. The swami ji was called to the palace where he quickly cemented his place alongside the other gods. The sanyasi told the Maharaja, 'The English are leaving India, I can see the writing on your forehead clearly. It's like the English letter "L". Which words begin with "L"? Lahore or Ladakh. Do not worry, Maharaja. With the blessings of Hanuman ji, your kingdom will extend from Lahore to Ladakh.'

The Maharaja fell for the mystical powers of his guru ji.

From that day onwards, Maharaja Hari Singh had two nemeses – Kak and Santdev. It was like fever with delirium, hail, and high water. The prime minister dispenses bad advice and the guru proposes an illusory future. The Maharaja hurtled headlong to his destruction. While all the native princes were joining the Indian union one after the other, he was dreaming of an independent Kashmir, straddling the distance between Pakistan and India, from Lahore to Ladakh. The English 'L' was glistening on his forehead. No joke!

Time and tide waits for none. Time had no patience for the Maharaja. Days and months went by unbidden. When Hari Singh's dream was finally broken, he opened his eyes to find his kingdom in turmoil and his capital almost slipping out of his hands. To save his skin and his kingdom from the Pakistani invaders, he was compelled to appeal to the Indian government for help. Prime Minister Nehru agreed to send troops on the condition that the Maharaja had public opinion on his side.

The kings of old used to run their kingdom as despots. When angry, they would burn somebody on stake and when pleased, they would bestow a kingdom along with a princess. Their subjects would pay the taxes without thinking and would suffer silently. Their retainers, though pauperized and starving, would still shout out weakly, 'Long live the king.'

Those days were gone. The time when the subjects would underwrite the ruler's extravagance was dead and gone. Now the people want to govern themselves. The ruler has to govern with the consent of the ruled. Nehru declared that only a popular leader would run the government in Kashmir.

Fittingly, Abdullah became the head of administration, though temporarily. Unfortunately, becoming the head of the province went to his head. Truth be told, Abdullah did not have any independent opinion. He adopted the opinion of his advisors and followed the path of his companions, wherever that led to. Bad company meant trouble. To that was added the lust for power, which knew no bounds. A number of wicked and selfish Muslims cozied up to him. They would surround him night and day like flies around a pail of milk and fill his ears with sinister advice.

Before long, Abdullah's mind became clouded again with delusion and conceit. From the heights of nationalism, his mind sank to the depths of communalism. His feet of clay stood revealed.

Abdullah nursed a grudge against Hari Singh. He could never forget that the Maharaja had thrown him into jail. But instead of making haste, he bade his time and waited for the opportune moment.

Initially, Abdullah demanded a ministerial government in Kashmir. Hari Singh would be the constitutional monarch, akin to the governor of an Indian state. A purely ornamental and non-functional post.

Sheikh Mohammad Abdullah finally became the prime minister of Jammu & Kashmir by sufferance of the Government of India.

Days went by. Hari Singh lost power, but retained his influence. The government employees were wont to looking up to the Maharaja as the sovereign. The illiterate peasants and workers would recall the Maharaja in times of trouble and hail him when delighted, out of old habit. That was not to the liking of the prime minister. By that time, the Indian troops had driven the invaders far afield. Abdullah deduced that the time was opportune and so he made his winning move. Hari Singh was checkmated.

Abdullah wrote to the Government of India that the people of the state do not want Hari Singh, so he would have to abdicate.

The news came as a blow to the Maharaja. He rushed to New Delhi. But whom would he turn to there? He met Nehru. Alas, he was not a friend of Hari Singh. Nehru had complete faith on Abdullah and upon democracy rather than on monarchy. Maharaja's plea fell upon deaf ears.

In the end, he had but to abdicate his throne against a pension. The young prince Karan Singh became the regent, that is the governor of Kashmir in the absence of his father. He was not even eighteen at the time.

Hari Singh had become the king even without being a prince. Now he lost his kingdom while still remaining a king. The letter 'L' preceded another English word – 'lost'. The guru Santdev was unaware of the word and Hari Singh had lost sight of it. Benighted Hari Singh!

With his state lost, Hari Singh went to Bombay and led a lonely existence there. From his window, the sea beach close by was visible. Countless waves kept crashing on the sand one after the other, ceaselessly. Hari Singh spent his empty days staring at them. Time and again, his mind would drift off to faraway lands, in spite of himself. There, on the mountaintop, golden sunlight glistened on silvery snow, leaves of the maple trees shimmered in the gentle breeze, and boatmen in their colourfully festooned shikaras sailed down the Jhelum, rowing with oars shaped like the ace of spade; on the edge of the Amirakdal Bridge, beggars begged for alms muttering, '*Miskin, miskin*'.

That land was lost to him forever. He would not set foot there ever again, the wretched king Hari Singh.

Acknowledgements

Jhelum Nodir Tirey is the augmented and fuller version of the essay, serialized in a periodical. It was undertaken at the request of the litterateurs Sri Sudhirchandra Sarkar and Sri Bishu Mukhopadhyay. The writer is immensely thankful to them.

The writer remembers with gratitude his indebtedness to all those books archives and government publications whose help was taken during research and those who had enlightened him about the unwritten chapters and 'behind the scenes' accounts of contemporary history from their personal experience and recollections. From that list, special mention must be made of: *Where Three Empires Meet* (E.F. Knight); *Jammu & Kashmir Territories* (Frederic Drew); *Gulab Singh* (K.M. Pannikar); *Reminiscences of a Bengal Civilian* (William Edwards); *Defending Kashmir* (Publications Division); *Condemned Unheard* (Unknown); *Despatches to the Secretary of State* (H.M. Durand); *History of the Sikhs* (Cunningham); U.N. Commissioners Report; *Mission with Mountbatten* (A. Campbell Johnson); *White Paper on Kashmir* (Government of India); Sheikh Mohammed Abdullah; Honourable J.M. Sadek; and Mrs Rajendra Singh.

1954

